My First Animal Library

Peacocks

by Cari Meister

Bullfrog Books

Ideas for Parents and Teachers

Bullfrog Books let children practice reading informational text at the earliest reading levels. Repetition, familiar words, and photo labels support early readers.

Before Reading

- Discuss the cover photo. What does it tell them?
- Look at the picture glossary together. Read and discuss the words.

Read the Book

- "Walk" through the book and look at the photos. Let the child ask questions. Point out the photo labels.
- Read the book to the child, or have him or her read independently.

After Reading

- Prompt the child to think more. Ask: Have you seen a peacock before? Was its tail fanned out?

Bullfrog Books are published by Jump!
5357 Penn Avenue South
Minneapolis, MN 55419
www.jumplibrary.com

Library of Congress Cataloging-in-Publication Data

Meister, Cari, author.
  Peacocks / by Cari Meister.
    pages cm. — (Bullfrog books. My first animal library)
  Summary: "This photo-illustrated book for early readers tells the story of a party of peacocks spending the day in the trees"— Provided by publisher.
  Audience: Age 5.
  Audience: K to grade 3.
  Includes index.
  ISBN 978-1-62031-168-4 (hardcover) —
  ISBN 978-1-62496-255-4 (ebook)
  1. Peafowl—Juvenile literature. I. Title.
QL696.G27M45 2015
598.6'258—dc23
                                    2014032084

Series Editor: Wendy Dieker
Series Designer: Ellen Huber
Book Designer: Anna Peterson
Photo Researcher: Casie Cook

Photo Credits: All photos by Shutterstock except: Dreamstime, 17, 18; Nature Picture Library, 6–7; Thinkstock, 1, 16–17, 20–21, 23tl.

Printed in the United States of America at Corporate Graphics in North Mankato, Minnesota.

Table of Contents

Fan Tail

What is in the tree?

It is a peacock!

He flies to the ground.

Peck. Peck.

He looks for seeds
and bugs.

He pecks with his beak.

He digs with his claws.

A bug! Yum!

beak ·····▶

9

Here comes a peahen.
Her colors are dull.

peahen

The male does a dance.
He fans his tail.
Wow!

Look at his feathers.
They look like eyes.

They shine in the sun.

crest

The peahen likes his dance.
She likes his feathers.
She likes his head crest.
Soon they have chicks.

chick

17

Koo-ooo! Koo-ooo!
A peacock calls.

He warns his party.

Danger is near.

The birds fly to the trees.

Now they are safe.

Parts of a Peacock

tail
Male peacocks have a long train of tail feathers. They fan them out to attract females.

beak
Hard mouthparts used to pick up food.

claws
Hard, horny nails on a bird's foot.

Picture Glossary

crest
The feathers sticking up on top of the peacock's head.

party
A group of peacocks, chicks, and peahens.

dull
Not shiny or colorful.

peahen
A female peacock.

Index

To Learn More

Learning more is as easy as 1, 2, 3.

1) Go to www.factsurfer.com

2) Enter "peacocks" into the search box.

3) Click the "Surf" button to see a list of websites.

With factsurfer.com, finding more information is just a click away.